The

WOMEN

Laine Cunningham

The Beautiful Book for Women

Published by Sun Dogs Creations
Changing the World One Book at a Time

Print ISBN: 9781946732705

Cover Design by Angel Leya

The

BEAUTIFUL

BOOK

SERIES

Align Your Passion With Your Purpose

All you are right now is all
you are meant to be right now.

Maturity arises at every age.

*Matriarchs see the future
in the present.*

*The balance of a woman's life
is embedded in a woman's desires.*

Position yourself
for the best view
of your life's landscape.

Map the treasures within
your heart and your mind.

If the enchanted tower
is a myth, then
build your own castle.

The strength of will
is greater than
the strength of force.

*To ensure victory,
compete with yourself.*

Trailblazers clear the way
for everyone.

The heartwood of a tree is
the strongest part of the trunk.

*Where diverse voices
overlap lies the fertile soil.*

A forest can withstand
more than a single tree.

One beehive can produce
sixty pounds of honey.

*A woman at peace
keeps peace
in the world.*

*Women know that
the light of dawn
illuminates every life.*

Whatever uplifts women
uplifts everyone.

"Princess" is a pejorative
only among
those who cannot
recognize nobility.

Beauty is an inner quality
that beautifies the world.

Even hummingbirds

occasionally rest.

Feelings are
a font of wisdom.

*Storms polish a
woman's brilliant sheen.*

*Every woman is
her own goddess.*

The alchemical symbol
for "woman"
combines the spiritual
and the material.

Womanhood is an attitude of strength.

Virginity is one stage of a continuum.

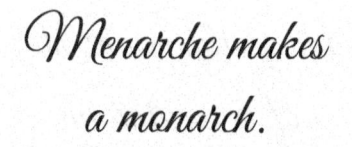

Menarche makes
a monarch.

Fertility is a state of mind.

*Each woman defines
her own femininity.*

Spinsters were independent spinners of wool.

*A woman should heed
her own opinion.*

*A woman can trust
her intuition.*

Anyone who wields shame
is an unworthy opponent.

The heart can be trusted
as much as the mind.

*The why of the matter is
intimately connected
to the who.*

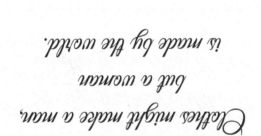

*Clothes might make a man,
but a woman
is made by the world.*

Biology provides a data set.
Everything else is up to you.

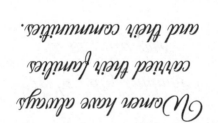

Women have always carried their families and their communities.

*To be fully genuine is
to be fully free.*

Empathy is a woman's most powerful tool.

*Speak with the confidence
your sisters need to hear.*

Courage lights
all wrongs.

Being silent is not the same as being still.

Those who intimidate
broadcast their fear.

*A woman frees
her sister's shackles
to be free of her own.*

*Rob stereotypes of power
by ignoring them.*

Women's worlds
incite change.

*To know
a woman's mind,
first know
a woman's heart.*

A woman's view of herself
is more revealing than
how others view her.

*Women tend to the light
they bring to the world.*

Women are invisible
only to those
who cannot perceive
their humanity.

*Pants? Dress?
Hell, yes!*

Each woman is a Venus
who rules her own heart.

*True equality arises
from true connection.*

*Equal pay arrives
with equal respect.*

Wholeness begins with wholeheartedness.

A woman's authenticity leads everyone to victory.

*A tough outer shell
shelters the tender flesh.*

Generosity is
glamorous.

Profound meaning arises
from profound friendships.

*Successful women tend
to their own needs.*

Sincerity is scintillating.

An act that enriches
a woman's inner world
also enriches
the wider world.

Wisdom is a sun that brightens the liveliness of day.

Love is a moon that softens the silence of night.

To prosper,

persevere.

Recognize
a woman's potential and
you will want
for nothing.

Women use what they
already have
to achieve even more.

Women will never
be invisible
to those
who can truly see.

Seemingly insignificant moments
coalesce into
a significant life.

NOVELS BY LAINE CUNNINGHAM

The Family Made of Dust

Beloved

Reparation

OTHER BOOKS BY LAINE CUNNINGHAM

*Woman Alone: A Six-Month Journey Through
the Australian Outback*

On the Wallaby Track

*Seven Sisters: Spiritual Messages from
Aboriginal Australia*

Writing While Female or Black or Gay

The Zen of Travel
The Zen of Gardening
Zen in the Stable
The Zen of Chocolate
The Zen of Dogs

The Wisdom of Puppies
The Wisdom of Babies
The Wisdom of Weddings

Bikes of Berlin
Necropolises of New Orleans I & II
Ruins of Rome I & II
Ancients of Assisi I & II
Panoramas of Portugal
Nuances of New York
Glimpses of Germany
Impressions of Italy
Altitudes of the Alps
Knights Through the Ages
Coast of California
Utopia of the Unicorn
Flourishes of France
Portraits of Paris
Tableaus of Tbilisi
Grandeur in the Republic of Georgia

The Beautiful Book of Questions
The Beautiful Book for Dream Seekers
The Beautiful Book for Rebels
The Beautiful Book for Women
The Beautiful Book for Lovers

Printed in February 2022
by Rotomail Italia S.p.A., Vignate (MI) - Italy